Trudy,
It was great seeing you again.
I hope you enjoy walking through these
experiences with Pa and me.

PASTOR *Charles Etta*

PASSION

AND

POETRY

Charles Etta Arkadie-Lucas

CHICAGO SPECTRUM PRESS
LOUISVILLE, KENTUCKY 40207

CHICAGO SPECTRUM PRESS
4824 BROWNSBORO CENTER
LOUISVILLE, KENTUCKY 40207
502-899-1919

Printed in the U.S.A.

10 9 8 7 6 5 4 3 2 1

ISBN: 1-58374-091-0

"A wonderful way to sum up a marriage of beautiful memories for others to view in print. God bless his memory."

Rev. and Mrs. T. H. Peoples
Lexington, Kentucky

"You truly displayed the love you have for C.B. We believe others will find joy in sharing this material."

Rev. and Mrs. J.L. Snardon
Louisville, Kentucky

"It is said that a good book is one that evokes a myriad of emotions. . .one that touches the depths of the soul while gently teasing the senses. One that causes you to think, smile, laugh, cry, reflect and wonder about what might have been. A good book challenges the intellect and stretches the thought process by stimulating memories.

Mom, you have done just that. . .Your memories of your life with Pa present a touching expose into the depths of your heart. Your poems reflecting the joy of life experienced with him and the lonely pilgrimage without him touches every aspect of emotion.

This book will serve as a catharsis for healing for those of us who deeply love and miss Pa. For while reading this book, we, too, will think, smile, laugh, cry, reflect and long to reach out and touch our beloved Rev. C.B. Lucas.

Well done, Mom; we, too, feel Pa is smiling and very, very happy".

Your son and daughter,
Gerald and Luevern Joiner
Roswell, Georgia

"Heartfelt and warming, the words cascade off the page and saturate the mind with a portrait of deep abiding love. Arkadie-Lucas gives the reader a glimpse of engulfing love, quenched that Father Time ripens and unfolds. A long simmering love, quenched with the soothing strength of C.B.

Lucas. Sneak peeks of lonely nights and misplaced days are reconciled by richness of a journey that is embraced by sensual, loving, endearing friendship that transcends between a husband and a wife."

Dr. Wanda Lott Collins
Minister, Professor, Author
Finchville, Kentucky

"Charles portrays the spirituality of her husband and their love for each other intertwines with the humor and passion that makes her love continue."

Nita West,
Poet
Hanover, Indiana

"Bravo! This poetry is beautiful, graceful and direct. It makes one ponder love and loss in a way that renews the spirit. It's everything that a good sermon should be."

Paula Robinson
Poet
Greensboro, North Carolina

Contents

Acknowledgments

I praise God for C.B., my husband of 44 years, the two beautiful offspring of whom we are proud, Ronald (Sandra) and Kelly Frances Lucas (Dana); our eight grandchildren, Christina, Raru and Sheri, Jamie, Jamail, Shaina, Lauren and Erin; Cecil and Erma Freeny, Arthur and Genella Saxton whom God added to our family.

I further offer praises for Charlie and Carrie Hill-Arkadie, my parents, whose love and enormous physical sacrifices yet humbles me, whose nurturing and encouragement were building blocks for a positive self-esteem and work ethic that enabled me to rise above the cotton fields; for my brothers: Lester (Ethel), Melvin (Mae Lene), Robert (Yvette) and Kelly (Katie) who further undergirded me and continue to do so; for Craig Marberry who, without knowing it, became my mentor; for Paula Robinson whose critiquing of these poems made a positive difference and for Termaine Shellman whose artistry gave additional life to numerous poems.

I owe much to my extended family, Rev. and Mrs. Thomas Lucas (Dana Mae), especially for their son, C.B. They welcomed me into their home providing me with sisters, Maxine Williams, Erma Jean Gray and one additional brother, Joseph (Alice). Their gathering around the breakfast table for devotion each Sunday morning was an established ritual that

C.B. and I adopted in our home as we embarked on a ministerial journey for Christ.

In all things, to God be the glory. It is He who enabled me to cut through a maze of emotions to write this reality and imaginative based poetry by reminding me that:

A cloud is but
a dark shadow that
covers a bright sunshine.

Dr. Clarence B. Lucas often boasted that he was one of two males in his graduating class at Daule High School in Cuero, Texas, his hometown. He was awarded a Bachelor of Science degree from Tillotson College, Austin, Texas, where he was inducted into the Omega Psi Phi Fraternity. After being discharged from the United States Air Force, he enlisted in its reserve as captain. Soon thereafter, he acknowledged his call to the ministry, enrolled at the Southwestern Baptist Theological Seminary, Ft. Worth, Texas, and was awarded the Bachelor of Divinity and Master of Religious Education Degrees.

Simmons Bible College later awarded him an Honorary Doctorate of Divinity Degree.

After pastoring briefly at Lone Star Baptist Church in Kaufman, Texas, he was employed to direct the Baptist Fellowship Center in Louisville, Kentucky. It was there he was called to pastor the Emmanuel Baptist Church where he served faithfully for 34 years until his death.

During his ministry he had occasion to assume leadership roles throughout the state of Kentucky and throughout a major portion of the United States. He had opportunities to worship and serve abroad through the Southern Baptist Convention, the Progressive National Baptist Convention and as an active participant in the Baptist World Alliance. His missions included service in various countries: Africa, the Bahamas, Trinidad and England.

His was joy resplendent in any capacity of work for the Lord. Known to give painstaking attention to details, while coordinating the Pastor's Conference for the last time, he indicated that he was extremely tired but quickly added, "I love it; I am enjoying every minute of it." As always, he was determined to work with diligence and faithfulness until the end of the workday. That he did.

> Words of wisdom
> Filtered down to man,
> "Take hold of the moment
> While you can."

Grooming

Simple Arithmetic

C.B. was led to
add his faith, subtract his ills
to multiply his blessings.

Birth of a Fashion

one boy's poverty
another boy's pleasure
become designer's
fashion statement

toasted knees
peeking through
pop art holes
stand out like
burned biscuits
on white
china plates

deep brown
crusty knees
don't fry
on mourner's
benches but
on fiery sand
while dragging
cotton sacks
under
parching sun

gaming with
prized marbles
scampering
on red clay
grind big
and bigger

pot holes
framing knees
like rays
sprouting
around the sun

one boy's poverty
another boy's pleasure
become designer's
fashion statement

The Call

Pear-shaped beads of sweat
plummeted down sun-burned cheeks
forming blinders over his eyes.

The roadmap on his shoulders gave testimony
of a sack laden with white billowy balls of cotton
trailing him quietly down cotton rows without end.

Silence succumbed to impulse as he implored,
"Mama, what'd happen if God called you
to preach and you just didn't do it?"

Her body unfolded to that of a statuesque lady.
Removing her calico bonnet, sweeping away the
sweat on her brow with the back of her hand
while holding his eyes captive, she calmly responded,
"Son, you won't never in this world be happy."

Lowering his eyes into the mouth of the cotton
sack, he vigorously scampered down the row plucking
buds of cotton and muttering to himself,
"Just about twenty-five minutes before sundown."

> *"before I formed you in the womb*
> *and before you were born*
> *I consecrated you a prophet in the nations."*
> > Jeremiah 1:5 (NIV)

(It really was there he first gave an indication of
his call to the ministry.)

Seminary Introduction (1955)

African? Islander?
No? A Texan?
Well, got one
garage
apartment.
One Colored's
already got
that one.
If you can find

a place to stay
with your folk,
we'll be mighty glad
to have you here
at the seminary.
Believe you'll be
the sixth one.
This here is a
mighty good school.

True Prosperity

The measure of
A great man's worth
Is not where he came from,
Nor his attainment of fame,
But the degree to which he fills
His vault with an abundance of
Faith, wisdom, knowledge
And fear of the Lord.

If the Lord delights
in a man's way,
he makes his steps firm;
though he stumble, he
will not fall,
for the Lord upholds him
with his hands.
Psalm 37:23 (NIV)

Mating

When kindred souls meet
hearts filled with rapture explode
bonding forever

Profile of the Spark

You caught my attention
when I saw you swagger
with that Texas stroll
jeans hanging loosely
on those low slung hips
moving cockily as if
the whole world awaited
your grand entrance.

Your mystical countenance
intrigued me, that slight frown
accenting piercing eyes
above spiraling cheekbones,
the irresistible dimple
flirtatiously posted mid-chin
compelling me to
probe deeply into
that dangerous fault
just before the earthquake.

Chemistry

That first encounter
So palatable
That first dance
Two gliders embarking
That first kiss
Rapture all aglow
That fusing chemistry
Mere clinging vines
Properties of a
Phenomenal change
Fused into one
Forevermore

Stalking the Chocolate

Grandma's bungalow
perched on a hill
overlooked fried grass
thirsting for a drink,
dried cockleburs standing
tall and vigilant in an attack mode
and my love gliding through the pasture.

Each morning my emaciated eyes waited
to feast on that slim chocolate morsel
who rhythmically pitched hay into
a circle of Holsteins flaunting designer's
coats of bold, black artsy prints
on white, furry backgrounds.

Chocolate morsels whetted my
appetite for penny peppermint canes.
Suddenly the country store with
eager zest beckoned me come
by way of my love's pasture.
Surely that chocolate nugget would
melt today and satisfy my palate.

A calf, barely one month old,
sporting a jagged black spot masking
one eye, announced my arrival
with a faint but pronounced, "moo."
My anxiety thermometer rapidly
arose to the acute danger zone.

My heart, pulsating ferociously, sought
temporary residence in my throat;
My body dutifully took up arms as a
loyal soldier defending her country.
My head veered neither right nor left
as I became a walking robot.

My peripheral vision captured
the pitchfork standing at attention among
stubby brown patches of grass as
my chocolate delicacy, flashing
a broad, winsome smile, moved
within range of my touch.

Triumphantly stuffing the
pennies into my pocket,
extending my arms to
encompass that big wad
of chocolate, I
gloated, "Won't need that
peppermint no more."

On Becoming

I am nothing

without you.

Pledge me this day

your infinite love

that I may

become.

The Subtle Approach

July 13, 1953

Dear Sir:

Please accept my application for a position as keeper of your heart. I am twenty-one years of age. I am somewhat of an amateur but will work diligently to perform satisfactorily. I am most anxious to begin as I feel time spent without this undertaking is worthless.

A personal interview may be arranged at your convenience, and, Sir, may I add that I hope your convenience is "soon."

Your immediate attention and response will be appreciated.

Respectfully,
(Miss) Charles Etta Arkadie

(C.B. and Charles Etta were married eleven months later. This letter was found among his papers after his death.)

Charles Etta Arkadie-Lucas

Impediment of Speech

I long to speak
of my great love for you
but my utterances
of adoration will
forever remain locked
in my bosom
lest you withdraw
from my rasping voice
in fear.

Look into my eyes
and hear my heart
speak so eloquently
of your charm
and of my desire
to claim you
as my betrothed.

Grant me the pleasure
of your response.
Fuel my light
by declaring
your love for me
and spiritual forces
will bear witness
of my sonnet
of love.

Metamorphosis- B and R

If I were a butterfly,
And you were a bee,
I'd display my beauty
For you alone to see.

Red, yellow, black wings
Flitting high above, then
Lighting right beside you
To convince you of my love.

All I ask off you, Dear Bee,
When for the pollen you dive,
Please return and just look at me
And cause me to come alive.

I'll alight on every flower
Where you've been, where you are.
I'll listen to your enchanting buzz;
I'll follow you near and far.

You'll give to me life's essence;
I'll be your courtly mate.
I'll watch as you make honey
And fly at your chosen gait.

The entire world will look at us
And think our mating funny,
I, the beautiful butterfly,
You, the maker of honey.

But, oh, we'll be so happy
As our differences blend,
You and me, me and you
Having bliss without end.

Never let differences
Your pathway dictate;
Accept the Lord's directions
And claim His choice of mate.

A Just-Right Blend

Reality, stooping to plant
a seed into my ear,
despairingly declared,
"Can't afford that
perfect wedding."

Fooled Reality!
Had a perfect wedding
anyway.
Just the bare essentials:
me, you and love.

Stars, streaming from eyes
beaming brightly with
anticipation,
transformed the ceiling
into a heavenly body
and thrift store clothing
into wedding apparel
fit for royalty.

The sky requested an audience as
lightning bolts vaulted, near and far,
illuminating the heavens.
Thunder, with its penetrating roar,
announced our joyful union
to an animated, heart-warming
 bunch of home folk
surrounding our place.

Hearts filled with rapture
gave ear
to distant foot movements
accompanied by primitive
drums and jubilant
ancestral songs

causing our spirited feet
to leap to heights
heretofore unknown.
What a wedding!
What a crowning event!

"Reality, hearts bound by love
will always soar beyond the
mere mundane
and take up residency in
a state of absolute bliss."

The Wedding Site
Yoakum, Texas

My Journal
June 1, 1954

Some reflections were never meant
To be recorded in black and white;
I merely blush when I recall
that blissful wedding night.

The Wedding Dance

Last night you visited me in my dream;
We were once again an Arthur Murray team.
I flashed you a smile and you, me, a grin;
We recounted the fun we had way back when
The highway our private ballroom became
The night I chose to share your name.
Centered in the highway we danced at midnight;
The man in the moon turned down the light
So we could gaze into each other's face
While experiencing the rapture of a warm embrace.
The highway was ours; no one came nigh
The natural ballroom under the starry sky.
The spell was broken by a deer hovering near
Who paused to witness the waltz of the year.
Our voices rang with high-pitched laughter;
We danced and danced 'til the morning after.
And years later when I'd entreat you to dance,
We'd spin 'round and 'round and giggle and prance
As we did the night I became your wedded wife
And sole dance comrade for the rest of your life.
By then... the dream began to fade away
And I braced again to face yet another day
Without your lead and loving touch,
Without the dance partner I revered so much.
As I grow older and my experiences become few,
I'll just turn back the clock, dream and dance along
with you.

(An apt description of our wedding night, June 1, 1954)

Chronology of a Portrait

Grandma's brush strokes
on a blank canvas
initiated a still life
of my eventful existence.
(Color it off-white.)

Painting the first motif
of the journey, she invited
"him" and family to a
get acquainted
supper.
(Color it green.)

Couldn't eat!
The dashing cutie's eyes
pursued me
dictating the palpitations
of my heart.
Smitten...I was.
(Color it red.)

Succumbing to love
I leaped over reasoning,
trussed up time into
tidy neat packages
and got married,
him and me.
(Color it white.)

Brushes boldly converted
delightful shapes

into exotic designs
giving rise to joy
and hilarious laughter.
(Color it sunshine yellow.)

The novelty of our haven
took back seat
to the grand entrances
of our son and daughter.
(Color it blue and pink.)

Dark, dank threatening clouds
filled empty spaces
without thought of effect
evoking pain and displeasure.
(Color it black.)

Touch-ups applied by Him
will complete the Master's
art show with our portraits
hanging side by side

in the ethereal gallery
of eternity.
(Color it heavenly blue.)

Joy Sublime

Each foreign encounter
Prepares one to elude
Camouflaged landmines
On the road to happiness

Love Defined

My love for you is like
stately calla lilies
coveting a northern breeze
which bids them sway
and dance like graceful
ballerinas.

like the savory grass seeds
changing garments
to become the essence of spring
under the caresses
of glittering raindrops.

like the alluring aroma
of fresh roasted coffee
whose fragrance stands still
long after the flame
is extinguished.

That's love,
true and
eternal.

Latitude

Upon accepting
His call
You asked
Naught
But I
Remain the me
That I was.
Unlike the
Chameleon,
Unmasked,
I sought
To display
Only His
Vivid colors,
Waving only
His banners
That I may
Become the me of
His choosing
Equipped for
Service
By your
Side.

Adapting

Succored

into Mother

Earth's

abode by

Bobolink,

Robin

sang songs

spliced with

anxiety

evolving

into joyful

sonnets

of praise

as Bob's nest

became

her habitat

of choice.

Happiness Is

The Hunter
treading among a colorful mosaic
of fallen leaves
sporting patched overalls and high-top
brogan shoes
walking laid-back like my pa
grandstanding his shotgun
pursuing jack rabbits all by myself for
the first time
developing a life-long passion
for hunting

The Fraternity
crossing the Omega Psi Phi line after
leading a dog's life of servitude
identifying my lowly status by
displaying a purple and gold paddle
twenty-four seven
lapping at big brothers' feet then
bonding triumphantly in fraternal love
as an equal
for the rest of my life

The Wife
holding my breath for a response to
 will you marry me
detecting the love and commitment
registered in her eyes
hearing a resounding yes

vowing our true love
'til death do we part

The Children
delighting marveling at the two
beautiful replicas produced
trembling at the awesome responsibility
to mold and support
commending each to Christ and us
to His leading
throughout parenthood

The Call
experiencing as never before a
forcible tug
running bargaining wrestling with
His call
stepping into His outstretched hands
in faith
depositing all earthly possessions in
the bank of eternity
committing my life to His service

The Reward
accepting unparalleled peace love joy and
security in Him
attaining happiness unsurpassed

Portraits of C.B.

Hold that pose!
Those penetrating eyes
are a lethal force.
Slightly part those lips
and chill.
Powerful!
You can let up, Man,
I got it!

Fashion Plate,
here's a mirror.
Brush those dark,
thick eyebrows
to be in perfect
symmetry with that
pencil-thin mustache.
Lean forward with
that winsome smile.
Just right!

Southwest,
Sport that wide-brimmed
cowboy hat
those snug fitting jeans
and brown cowboy boots
with toes curling skyward.
Stroll toward me
with slow threatening
"home on the range" steps.

Freeze! Gotcha!
Tex, that's all right!

CEO,
How about a pensive working
pose sitting at your desk?
Sorry, I want a picture
of you at work, not
that sculptured pile of litter.
Wait; straighten your tie;
give Pierre Cardin his due.
Answer the phone while
sporting a thoughtful look.
Hold it right there.
Not bad! Not bad.

Negotiator,
Just be natural!
Pat the back of your head
as you usually do
and assume an
imploring stance.
Lock eyes with the victim.
I'll snap when I
hear you say, "Well...."
Absolutely superb!

Hey, you're not bad,
A perfect model
With natural charisma.
Ever thought of
acting? modeling?
Yeah, I know;
you're on a mission
for the Lord. Let me know
if you change your mind.

Sentimental Recollections

Some days I place you
in a closet and
ask you there to stay;
other days I tenaciously
embrace you and lament
when you go away.

Hometown Treasures
(Cuero, Texas)

Standing stoically
at the curve to
the pecan house,
a grand old oak
proudly spread its
massive wings
to embrace all
magnetized by
its grandeur.

Pausing within
the oak's shadow,
I recalled flash bulbs,
you, me smiling
against the picturesque
backdrop of the
awesome proud oak
so overpowering
we each looked like
lone startled ants
on bold flowered
tablecloths.

The squirming curve,
with magnetic force,
propelled me forward
as a portly old gentleman,
with a welcoming smile,
beckoned me enter his

one-room cottage bursting
with Texas-sized pecans.

Scrutinizing my face with
an uncanny perception,
he pointed toward the window
framing the grand old oak,
"We've weathered many 'a. storm
'cause the man upstairs' umbrella
hovers over us. Lady, I expect
there's plenty room for you."

A tender oak branch peering
through the window pane bowed regally
as its fluttering leaves whispered
a gentle farewell.

Basking in the warmth of
their affection, sensing
your presence beside me,
I drove boldly with one hand
while five other fingers deftly delved
into sacks of gigantic Texas pecans,
igniting an explosive smile,
giving birth to a new resolve,
as the radio belted out
the timely melody,
"Tomorrow."

comradery

strolling observing
the wonders of nature
you pause
grasping my hand
that I may walk
by your side

shopping bargaining
for rare finds
I observe
your stance
smiling willing
the malls
to shut down

projecting babbling
like a tightly-wound
alarm clock
evoke nothing
but your
attentive ear

reminiscing reveling
at your endearment
I hold fast
my comrade
of yesteryear
my center
of today

My Chameleon

You rang my bell
Each time you called my name.
Your injection of "luv"
On the "do, re mi" scale gave
Rise to fresh musical scores.

On snow-clad wintry evenings
Your receptive body
Elevated its thermostat to
Pacify my perpetually
Cold shimmering feet
Until our space registered
In the comfort zone.

Misadventure often sneaked
Into our tranquil lives.
My pride blossomed at
Your bold transformation
Into a giant octopus with
Tentacles overpowering
Each monstrous obstacle.

When my piercing screams
Broke the Richter Scale,
You became my knight
Fortified with armor and
Resolve to extinguish
Household invaders.

When I became unstrung,
You tempered my anxiety
With your Louisiana Stew and
Sedating counsel to relax.

Daily I savor your memory
And give God the praise.

Pilgrimage and Memories—
Lone Star Baptist Church
(Kaufman, Texas)

Miles of serene rustic prairie
Stretch forth rural arms
Beneath gold crested oaks to
Extend a gracious reception

Jagged road signs, jarring
Recollections buried deeply
In my revered treasure chest
Of memory, bid my spirit
Return to its roots.

Familiar faces and voices,
Seasoned and youthful,
Living and dead, parade before
Me babbling words of good will.

My spirit catapults to mountainous
Heights at your powerful delivery of
His word to the parade's spirited
Chorus of "Hallelujah," "Amen."

Stepping out of the '60's capsule
I smile as the rear view mirror
Reflects each loving haloed face
Journeying alongside me.

Basking in each crown of light,
I gratefully conclude:
 I am because
You and they
Are.

Eyes in Retrospect

A breathtakingly beautiful
array of wild flowers
clothed in garments
befitting royalty
bids us welcome
to the garden of
memories.

Dewberries, firm,
faintly red to
soft, fleshy black,
clamor for
attention
with their sweet,
colorful appeal.

Blue bonnets,
buttercups
cushion Easter
Bunny's eggs;
jelly pails
overflowing with
purple, wild grapes
coax blue teeth to
artfully announce
their abundance.

Stones, tall, jagged,
flat, sculptured
beg for recognition

as works of art.
Low lands overgrown
with ears bent
listen to tenants'
tales of intrigue,
survival and triumph.

Unleashed hearts
smiling, reflecting
on these grandiose
scenes of yesterday,
post each snapshot
as a memoir
for our posterity.

The TKO

A wasp got into the kitchen today;
I figured you'd know what to do.
So I did what you'd expect;
I screamed and waited for you.

But, Papa, you can't come no more
And I just can't go to bed.
Instead of sleeping peacefully,
I'd have eons of nightmares instead.

Papa, do I really haveta fight this thing?
You know I'm too scared to do that!
I can no more swat a household fly
Than the tail of a tailless cat.

So, Papa, I'll haveta get that broom
And whack that sucker dead
To terminate its ramblin'
and flirtin' around my head.

Hon, I beat and beat and beat it;
Every time I knocked it down
It pranced on the floor and then arose
Like Mike Tyson for another round.

I gave that bugar one good smash;
Into hot dishwater it fell;
I felt sorry for it but instinctively knew
It was either his or my living hell.

I didn't feel good about what I did;
I just knew what had to be wrought;
I await recognition of valor from you
For fightin' where you should've fought.

The Mall Walk

Sculptured horses spout steady streams of
diamond-studded water into the wishing well.

Tired-faced and decrepit old men huddle together
over coffee rehashing the exploits of their youth.

A portly couple bedecked in matching attire
parade as drum majors of physical prowess.

Swinging tightly clasped hands, teenagers stroll
oblivious to all but the grandeur of each other.

Wide-strapped suspenders support baggy pants of a silver-
haired gentleman toddling like a babe taking his first steps.

Salesclerks, mimicking disoriented mice, race against
the clock whose finger menacingly points toward ten.

Each observation evokes from me a response;
I turn to speak....you're not there.
Reality flaunts its nakedness;
I must walk
alone.

My Saint Nick

Admiring the scenery while passing by
I saw St Nick wickedly wink his eye.
I thought, "Surely this just cannot be
That St Nick's making a pass at me."
I looked more closely at that chocolate face.
He looked like the guy I once embraced,
Same billowy eyebrows, same dancing eyes,
Same romantic stare under that St Nick disguise.

When I saw him beckon me to get in line,
I immediately leaped behind number nine.
Both parents and children gave me a dirty stare
As if to say, "How dare you cut in there!"

St Nick hurriedly bade number nine goodbye;
Once again he flirtatiously winked his eye.
He instructed me to sit on his soft, pudgy knee
And list what I wanted under the Christmas tree.

I looked more closely at St Nick's face.
Could it possibly be the one I long embraced?
Feeling quite foolish, I whispered in his ear,
"Lend me the service of your fastest reindeer."

St Nick and I kissed, impetuously kissed some more;
The bystanders reacted with a distasteful roar.
I hurriedly departed without a look behind
At the startled children still waiting in line.

I know I looked odd; folk just have to understand;
St Nick wasn't a stranger; I really knew that man.
I can't explain what happened; just remember this;
If I declare I love a man, I certainly know his kiss.

I don't need no more St Nicks to make promises to me;
I plan to junk all gifts planted under my tree.
Christmas will be complete when St Nick holds me tight
And promises to be with me each and every night.

The Wishing Well

I pitched a copper penny
Into an old wishing well;
I gazed ever so intently
'til I saw just where it fell.

Then I tightly closed my eyes
And lifted my heart in prayer;
I wished as my eyes opened
I'd find you standing there.

I opened my eyes ever so slowly,
Not a sign of you to be found;
I didn't register disappointment;
I knew you were still around.

You're here in my recollections;
There's so much to recall,
The journeys we took together,
The last to Niagara Falls,

Each time I hear my name called
In such a special way,
Each time I view the setting sun
We shared at the close of a day.

I recall the awe we both felt
As we observed his creation;
At the sight of a lone loping deer,
Our voices rang in adulation.

Each time you knew that I was ill,
You took over as never before.
When impatient words leaped from my lips,
You'd gently close the door.

You became an integral part of me,
Though I didn't know it then,
The extent of your very being as
My companion, lover and friend.

I feel your presence beside me;
Your prodding edges me on.
Valiantly I now face the future
Without dread of the burst of dawn.

Observers often implore me
The secret of my confidence to tell;
I simply smile and say, "My dear,
It's the penny thrown into the well.".

The Spoof

Pa, I'm not irreligious;
This I write is just a spoof.
When I catch up with you in heaven,
I'll demand you show me proof
That the good Lord had you destined
To join Him on that fateful day,
That you didn't tire of work down here
Begging time-out to feast and play.
If that be true, Dear Light of Mine,
Our reunion there won't be quite so fine.
You, Dear Angel, won't navigate or fly
'cause you'll be sporting a big, black eye.

Closure

Life
As I see it
Is but a bucket
Waiting
To be filled
Or waiting
To be spilled

The Façade

Our days together passed so very fast;
Does anything good ever last?
What happened to our yesterday
With pleasant recollections ever so dear
When abundant living overshadowed each tear
And life was jubilant and gay?

Could it be in nostalgia we
Pluck dead leaves from our living tree
And cast them into a forgotten heap,
Keeping our tree forever green,
Unpleasantries then are never seen,
Propelling ecstasy into a bountiful leap?

Dance Impulse
(1997 Cruise)

I want
to sail in your arms
across the dance floor
and let the sea breeze
chart our course.

I want to
rest my head
on your shoulder,
to hear your heart palpitate
in response to mine,
to giggle once more while
spinning into a solo act.

I want
to be imprisoned
in your secure arms,
to create our own private island
in the midst of a crowd,
to synchronize our steps and
become mesmerized as one.

I want
to close my eyes,
to dare to dream
of numerous tomorrows,
to just shut out the world
and follow your lead
until the band stops playing
and we complete
our last dance.

The Inquiry

My Lord, is it really true
You're allowing me to rest?
I've not always been faithful
Nor have I always done my best.

But I never stopped struggling, Lord
To preach your holy word
Though, at times, it seemed to me
The message was not even heard.

To be very frank, Dear Lord,
That's when my soul would tire,
Then I'd ask the Holy Spirit to work
And give me a renewed desire.

With restored vigor I'd hungrily delve
Into your Holy Word so
The love that dwelled within me
Could be seen as well as heard.

Come around another Sunday
When a changed life I'd see,
I'd weep for joy that the Holy Spirit
Had done its work through me.

So now you say, "C.B. come home;
Lay your staff and burdens down.
You've multiplied the talents received;
Enter these gates and claim your crown."

Just as I am,
Dear Lord,
I come.

An Awakening

So still he lies
Undisturbed by
The pilgrimage
Of onlookers
Trudging by
And pausing
To assess
The state
Of the dead.
They peer into
The tranquil face
With terse expressions
That belie unuttered words.
Yet he lies
Oblivious to
Sounds, songs,
Resolutions,
And
Piercing wails
Not for him
But
Reflectively
For man's inevitable,
Placid state.
The mourners
Then
Somberly
Move on.

Time

Time unassumingly creeps forward
Moving silently toward infinity
With a scythe-like blade
Hewing all within its course
Without a backward glance
At its clean-shaven path
Giving rise to the destiny of all.

Songs of Sorrow

One in dire sorrow
Will pretend it is not so
and cry in private

Lost

I am no longer me;
I am the person that was.
Observe the turbulence
Concealed in my plastered smile;
Behold my measured steps
As uncertain as a toddler
Propelled to an object
Of which he knows not.
Hear the guttural sounds uttered
As a babe imitating
The confused mixture
Of syllables around him.
My person is abandoned.
My persona, displaced.
A hollow tree, I am.
So now, I search
For me;
I search; I search
For me.

The Puzzle

I am a tripod
On which the worlds stand;
I am an ocean,
The alternative to land.
I am the bark
That surrounds a tree;
I am an enigma
In search of me.

Spring on Hold

Hold back the spring
Until my broken heart
Is mulched
In preparation
For living.

Put a cap
On the daffodils
Until my eyes
Fully comprehend
Their majestic beauty.

Let each blade of grass
Deny its ability to prevail
Though caressed by
Gentle spring showers.

Let each statuesque tree
Covet its bare frame
And protest the parasitic
Invasion of foliage,
Of birds procreating.

Hold back the spring
Until the time is ripe,
Until reasoning is inclined
To accept the order
Of God's universe
And my broken heart
Is mended.

Ignorance Ain't Bliss

How was I supposed to know
that our Datson B210 was addicted
to water? It got real thirsty and
stated matter-of-factly," I quit,"
leaving me stranded on the
Gulf Coast with only seagulls
as companions.

Why'd you insist on taking
over the steering wheel when we
 got to big metropolitan areas?
You strangled my self-confidence.
Now who's gonna drive for me?

Can you believe I approached
a stranger on our street and asked,
"Sir, will you please come kill
a giant spider who won't let
me out my own back door?"
Why didn't you make me
kill my own bugs?

And all those bills!
Wonder why those businesses
don't just get together and send
them all at one time? A bill
here, a bill there...Sometimes
I simply ignore them for a spell.
I expect my credit rating's done
gone down the drain.

And don't let me hire someone
to cut down a tree, paint the patio,
put a lock on a door, repair the car
 or do anything. They ask how
much I have in the bank
and take it all.

And so, here I am, Papa,
helpless and ignorant,
ignorant and helpless
but eternally grateful
to you for the forty-four
years of reprieve.

The Conquest

Bleeding hearts
Form a ne'er ending stream
Fueled by the savage storm.
Turbulent waters drift
unabated in its quest
For tranquility.

Desolate hearts
Echo drums of distress
With each pounding heartbeat.
Densely grown blades of despair
Threaten to camouflage paths
To freedom.

Weary hearts
Mobilize their spirits
and abolish the gloom
Of dense foliage
Overshadowing the land,
Triumphantly reclaiming
Life's passion to live

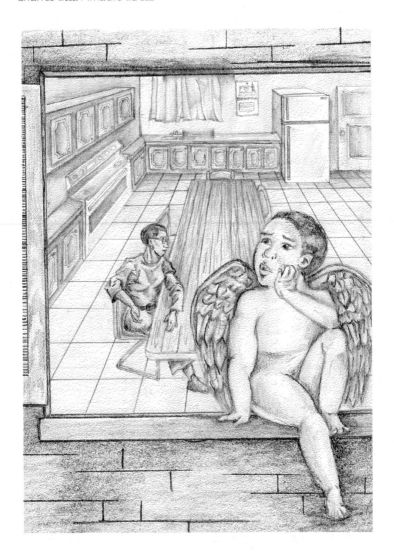

Valentine Day

Cupid
Won't lodge
On my
Breakfast
Table
This year.

Too bad!
Wish he'd
Told me
What to
Do with
The emp-
ty space.

Christmas without You

Dreaming?
Of a white Christmas?
Without you?
My snow is now
Sculptures of slush
Muted with grime
From stampeding autos.
Christmas glitter
Dulls my eyesight;
Silver bells ring out
Joyless, holiday tunes
And Santa is but
A pompous
Façade.
Dreaming?
Of a white Christmas?
Without you?

Growth and Demise

Our faces registered delight
Our eyes danced and
Our hearts beat euphorically
As we laid claim to our house.

The snow-covered trees bowed
In courtly splendor to welcome us.
A squirrel scampered up a bare tree
And stood at attention to greet us.
Our arms and hearts locked as
Reality supplanted our dreams
When we moved into our house.

Bidding the snows farewell,
Saplings of dogwoods we planted
Gave birth to fragrant blossoms
Forming gigantic bouquets with hues
Of pink, white, rose and lavender,
A portrait that broadened our smiles
And transformed our faces
Into replicas of delight.

The tulip bulbs produced
A battalion of proud soldiers
Bedecked in colorful splendor.
Having escaped from captivity,
They stood vigilant and regal;
We spoke not a word.
Our rejuvenation, joy and pride
In the outgrowth of our handiwork

Were registered in our eyes.
Our countenance mirrored
Our heart's satisfaction.

A tiny seedling became a giant tower
Whose boughs were a barometer of our
Graceful maturation together.
This green giant bounded upward
As if to caress the billowy clouds.
Our steps strove to keep abreast
As our house monitored
The friendly competition.

We relished the security, comfort
And solitude our house afforded.
We pondered the journal recorded by our house
Of secrets never to be revealed,
Of ecstasies never to be reborn.
The love for our abode and each other heightened
And we embraced as only lovers can..in our house.

Now they ask about our names.
Were they joined by "and" or by "or"?
They appraise our house
Whose luster is now diminished
And is a woeful reminder
Of the aroma that lies dormant,
Of the lost exuberance seasons bring
Of the towering cedar that no longer
Gauges our growth by its boughs.

With palpitations invading my heart;
With contortions assailing my entire being,

Through a thin veil of tears,
I perused the deed...
Only one name.
Just one name.

Zero

I dream not,
I perceive not,
I desire not,
I produce not,
'cause
you're not
beside me;
therefore,
I cannot
'cause
without
you
I am
not.

Free at Last

Peace eludes me.
My heart agonizes
As though pierced
By a fiery dart.

From wearied eyes,
Tears flow freely
As though leaping
From Niagara Falls.

Futile utterances,
Incoherent words
Tumble from my lips
In language
unknown to man.

I inquire of the sages;
Their counsel fails me.
I implore friends
Who listen but
Do not hear.

In utter dismay
I frantically cry out,
"Father of the Universe,
This day grant me peace."

Joy swiftly bursts forth
From its prison cell
And berates me saying,
"Next time, try Him first."

The Search

Is it o.k. to
blurt out, "Where is my husband"
though no one hears?

Would I be viewed as
suspect to call his name while
casting my eyes heavenward?

What emotions would
my flush of tears and red eyes
evoke from a stranger?

When will this sentence
of pain, grief and unrest cease
to lay hold of me?

Your sun will never set again
and your moon will wane no more;
the Lord will be your everlasting light
and your days of sorrow will end.
                                    Isaiah 60:20 (NIV)

…weeping may remain for a night
but rejoicing comes in the morning.
                                    Psalm 30:5 (NIV)

The Reunion

Papa, Mother Nature, pregnant
With life is issuing in a new birth.
 Blankets of blue bonnets
Form a sea of dashing waves.
Oceans declare a moratorium
On waters lapping the shores
In favor of spring's wanderlust
To cover the countryside
With varying hues of
Blue and green.

The dogwood tree's blossoms
Burst open like fluffy balls of cotton.
Its pink and yellow offspring are enjoined
To soar upward to the heavens
Spreading beauty along the way,
To lay claim on its space
Among clouds of kindred souls,
To rest throughout eternity
Having fulfilled its mission below.

My eyes, beholding the flight of
Mother Nature's offspring,
Cascade bold tears rushing
Like waterfalls with their
Comforting melodies
Of quiet joy.

Like the dogwood blossoms,
My spirit will ascend to the heavens

To reside among angelic forces
And joyfully join hands
With my love in
Adoration and praise.

Acceptance

Each experience is
A part of the Master's plan
To equip one for service

Life Cycle

A seed is planted;
it germinates.
A seedling grows;
it matures.
The plant blooms
bearing fruit,
blessing others.
It dies
as He wills.

There is a time for everything,
and a season for every activity
under heaven:
a time to be born
and a time to die
a time to plant and
a time to uproot.
                    Ecclesiastes 3:1-2 (NIV)

Let There Be Light

After a fierce, tumultuous storm,
a beautiful rainbow of promise
adorns heaven's gallery.

After a pitch-dark, moonless night,
dawn, in a gentle and timely manner,
escorts in daylight.

After a loved one gallantly
steps off the stage,
God, the director, remains
until the final curtain is drawn.